T0065181

DEVELOP *YOUR* SPIRITUAL BUSINESS

Gerald Melton

authorHOUSE®

AuthorHouse™
1663 Liberty Drive
Bloomington, IN 47403
www.authorhouse.com
Phone: 833-262-8899

Published by AuthorHouse 11/10/2022

ISBN: 978-1-6655-7588-1 (sc)
ISBN: 978-1-6655-7587-4 (e)

Print information available on the last page.

Scripture quotations marked NIV are taken from the Holy Bible, New International Version®. NIV®. Copyright © 1973, 1978, 1984 by International Bible Society. Used by permission of Zondervan. All rights reserved. [Biblica]

This book is printed on acid-free paper.

CONTENTS

DEVELOP YOUR SPIRITUAL BUSINESS

PROLOGUE: DEVELOP YOUR SPIRITUAL
BUSINESS TO FULFILL THE CALL OF GOD
IN YOUR LIFE.

START WITH AN ATTITUDE CHANGE

How can we begin our spiritual business? We can get up and do something about it! We can stop feeling helpless over our condition. These are attitude changes which will change our actions. We see in Proverbs 6:6-11 (NIV) that it's essential that we have an attitude change over the work we are responsible for as a Christian.

Why must we have an attitude change over the work we are responsible for as a Christian? Let's see why we must have an attitude change over the work we are responsible for as a Christian.

Having an attitude of taking initiative is critical for exercising our gifts. Proverbs 6:6-7 says, "Go to the ant, you sluggard; consider its ways and be wise! It has no commander, no overseer or ruler…" If we examine these verses; we will see that the ant works without someone telling it what to do; it works with no leader over it; yet it wastes no time in preparing its food supply for the winter! We must initiate the knowledge of our gifts and put them to use! No-one will do this for us! It is up to us to exercise our gifts! The verse says to go to the ant! We need to go to our mentors and put their example into practice. We need to practice the advice of doing something with our life! The ant has no commander! We must learn to be leaders over our own personal inventory of gifts, talents, abilities, and resources. The question we must ask ourselves is, "When will we begin to exercise our gifts and purpose on a regular basis?" How long before we take responsibility over our own work in the Lord. If we are a body builder; we know that if we stop exercising, then we will lose the progress we made. It is like this spiritually! We must exercise our gifts! If we don't change our attitude to take initiative, then we won't fulfill the work God intended for us.

We must begin to examine our gifts and look at how we can use it for Gods glory.

Having an attitude of being diligent is critical for obtaining the harvest. Proverbs 6:8 says, "Yet it stores it's provisions in summer and gathers its food at harvest." The ant wastes no time getting to work to obtain its needed harvest. And it lacks not; and its colonies grow and expand. The bible says that the ant stores its provision. Diligents to work for God is essential for our eternal harvest. The ant also gathers at harvest. It does not sleep at harvest when work must be done! It does not procrastinate; if it did it would die out; it must labor. A worker on the job understands this concept: if we won't work, we shouldn't eat. There is a danger in missing out on harvest because you are not willing to work. If we apply ourselves to obtain the fruit; then we will obtain an eternal result, or a lasting result.

Having an attitude of staying watchful for opportunity is critical to be faithful with our stewardship. Proverbs 6:9 says, "How long will you lay there you sluggard? When will you get up from your sleep?" If we will not get up, then we cannot be open to spot and receive opportunity! We must begin to go out and look for opportunity before she will come to our door. Without opportunity we won't have anything to be faithful with. Solomon asks us how long will we sleep? How long before we take initiative and go out with all our ability and put those gifts to work? We are made for that! Solomon asks us if we will get up. We must change our attitude and disposition to, "I'm going to work!" Be ready to correspond and take advantage of opportunity. Go to work and make it happen. There is no magic to a 9 to 5 worker; he/she just makes it happen. We are called to faithfully work. If we won't go out and do the work of God; we will miss our reason for living. We must put our gifts to work to obtain the reward from God.

Having an attitude of determination is critical to avoid the danger of apathy towards God's assignments for us. Proverbs 6:10-11 says, "A little sleep, a little slumber, a little folding of the hands to rest; and poverty will come upon you like a bandit and scarcity like an armed man." We need determination to get out of the state of slumber: Slumber and waiting leaves us destitute of God's blessings. Scarcity both physical and spiritual will come upon us: a spiritual desolation. Solomon mocks about our slumbering. We must get up and out of our sleep. He went on to say that poverty and scarcity will come upon the lazy like a bandit and like an armed man. Wicked propensities will overthrow the things that God intended for us if we let laziness and procrastination guide us. Neglect of the gifts leads to their undoing. God intends that we jump on His assignment for us: make it happen! Can we change our apathy to determination? If we will do this; God will bless our efforts.

We therefore need to change our attitude over our work; then we will accomplish much for God and the Kingdom; and we will lay a rich foundation for the time to come.

ESTABLISH THE RIGHT FOUNDATION

The foundation is essential to building a solid building. Without a solid foundation the building is unstable. Without a solid foundation the building is not usable. Establishing the right foundations is crucial to our spiritual work. In Matthew 7:24-25 (NIV) we see that it is essential that our spiritual business is built on the right foundation. Why is it essential that our spiritual business is built on the right foundation? Let's see why it is essential that our spiritual business is built on the right foundation.

Hearing and practicing Gods Word is a solid foundation. Matthew 7:24 says, "Therefore everyone who hears these words of mine and puts them into practice is like a wise man who built his house on the rock." If we will begin to undertake a spiritual work, then we must have a foundation that can support such a work. This and any valid spiritual endeavor start by hearing the Words of Jesus. We must seek God on how to apply His Word through the opportunities to use our gifts. Jesus spoke of hearing His Words. We must start on the only foundation worth building on which is Jesus Christ. If we put His Words into practice, we will have to search out the best ways to apply our life abilities to fulfill Gods Word; then we'll be on solid Rock. As we acquire the teaching and implications of bible truth and put them into practice: our work will survive and thrive the storms of adversity. Without Christ as our foundation; as is taught in scripture; our work will be or will become illegitimate. An illegitimate work will not be recognized. There is a great danger in seeking to do a public work or social work without Jesus as our foundation. But if we seek the Lord for the godly foundation; it's probable; if we don't quit; that God will build our work.

Our Work will face heavy storms; so, it needs to be built on the solid foundation. Matthew

7:25a says, "The rain came down, the streams rose, and the winds blew and beat against that house ..." If we build on Jesus Christ as the foundation for our work and spiritual business; we can endure the storms! It is worth the effort to build our spiritual work and business on biblical truth. Know for sure that heavy storms will blow against our works to see what will stand and fall! Jesus spoke about the rains coming down. Rain can erode even the hardest earthly stones over time. But Jesus Christ is the heavenly Rock. He cannot be corrupted. We see that streams rose; winds blew and beat against the house. Many forms of offense will batter against our spiritual business. The only one able to handle the storms of life is the Creator and Savior Jesus Christ. Have you ever been caught in a major storm without having your weather gear? You, in this situation, could freeze or die. That is why we need a foundation able to stand the impact.

Our work will stand when built on the solid foundation. Matthew 7:25b says, "Yet it did not fall because it had its foundation on the rock." If we proceed to build our life work on Jesus Christ; our work will be established. Jesus is the impeccable foundation. Jesus is the solid Rock in which rain cannot penetrate. Proceed to build; and to build on the Rock. Recall the verse said that the house did not fall. Our work or business can last by Jesus as the foundation and source of it. That is because our work has Jesus as the foundation; and we are exercising the vision God laid out for us in His Word. Imagine us establishing a work in people that lasts for eternity: that is God's Will. It takes effort to learn to hear and discern Gods voice and attempt to build accordingly. We can choose our own way; or an admired friend; but that is not building on Jesus Christ. We will have friends that we can trust if you seek out Gods way.

Let us build our spiritual business on Jesus Christ; and our work will endure life's storms and continue a long time.

DISCOVER AND EXERCISE YOUR GIFTS

How can we use your abilities? We must discover and list those abilities; then we focus on a mission statement to put those gifts into motion. God makes it clear in Romans 12:3-8 (NIV) that you have ability and potential. I want to express in this study that it is necessary that we exercise our abilities according to the differing gifts God has given us. Why is it necessary that we exercise our abilities according to the differing gifts God has given us? Let's see why it is necessary that we exercise our abilities according to the differing gifts that God has given us.

It is necessary that we exercise our abilities because God has granted us a measure of faith.

Romans 12:3 says, "For by the grace given me I say to every one of you: do not think of yourself more highly then you aught, but rather think of yourself with sober judgment, in accordance with the measure of faith God has given you." Our ability to believe and exercise confidence in our abilities and resources has all come from God! We are cautioned; then, to do all things humbly and in honor in the Lord. We are to think soberly and biblically if we will please God. This passage warns us not to think more highly then we should about ourselves. All we possess has come from God; so, we shouldn't think its some great thing we do. Rather we are to think with sober judgment. We need to think in biblical terms. We are to do all this according to the measure of faith given us. God gave us faith and gifts and He expects us to use all for the kingdom sake. We must not waist our stewardship over our faith and gifts. There was a parable about the unjust steward who lost his stewardship; let's not let unfaithfulness cause that to happen to us. We must look for every opportunity to use our gifts for Gods work.

It also is necessary that we exercise our abilities because the body of Christ needs us to share our gifts. Romans 12:4-5 says, "Just as each of us has one body with many members, and those members do not have the same function, so in Christ we who are many form one body, and each member belongs to all the others, according to the grace given us." You are a complete unit: and in Jesus Christ; His followers are called the church or the body of Christ; and the body is one! We belong to each other! Only by Jesus leading through grace will we be able to share what we have with the body of Christ. Each member does not have the same function. Like our body; our hand is a subunit of the body; and it is different and has a different purpose then the foot or eye. We who are many forms one body verses 4-5 says. Each part of our bodies relies on the other parts: it's the same in Jesus Christ. Our future glory relies on our kinetic support to the body of Jesus Christ today. Jesus said to obey the command to love one another if we do love Him. The body of Christ is essential to our place in eternity. If we love the body of Christ and support Jesus Christ cause; we lay a good foundation.

Again, it is necessary that we exercise our abilities because it is a grace granted by God.

Romans 12:6 says, "If a man's gift is prophesying, let him use it in proportion to his faith." All our gifts operate by faith: God has given both the gifts and is the author of our faith. God expects us to be faithful; and if we neglect this grace then we will be the loser. All the gifts have come from God. And the bible says for each man to, "let him use it (his/her gift.)" God expects us to use our gifts for His glory. We are to do so in proportion to our faith. God wants us to use those gifts according to balance; recognizing Him as the author of all our works in Christ. We must give God glory for all good things given us and the good things God allows us to do. We can lose our grace and the ability to use our gifts if we neglect them and disregard God! We must be zealous for Gods work; and we will please God in the use of those gifts.

It is also necessary that we exercise our abilities because each person has a specific gift(s). Romans 12:7-8 says, "If it is serving, let him serve; if it is teaching, let him teach; if it is encouraging, let him encourage; if it is contributing to the needs of others, let him give generously; if it is leadership, let him govern, diligently; if it is showing mercy, let him do it cheerfully." God has given gifts to each believer: Serving, teaching, encouraging, giving, leadership, mercy, and others. It's our responsibility to discover, grow in, and daily exercise that gift. The passage speaks of serving; a ministering to others needs; this is the whole purpose of our purpose. Each gift or ability should be used to serve others. Would we discard a discipline we learned in college? Neither do we discard any gift we recognize that God has given us. God has given us these gifts to support and build others up! When we bypass the opportunity to use our gift or ability; we waist and opportunity to have that gift established in heaven. We must be very observant to catch and take advantage of every opportunity to use our gifts to help others. If we do these things, we will lay a sure foundation for the time to come.

God has given each one of us different gifts and it's up to us to discover, develop, and use them in all of life.

KNOW AND LIVE OUT YOUR PURPOSE

Do we know our purpose? Have we made a list of our abilities, skills, and talents? Have we located our resources? If we put in the time, we can be prepared to live out a life of purpose. We see in Titus 2:6-8 (NIV) that we can know how our life's conversation should be. How should our life conversation be? Let's see how our life's conversation should be.

Our life's conversation should be a demonstration of self control. Titus 2:6 says, "Similarly, encourage the young men to be self-controlled." In our example to others; we can set the tempo for discipline, action, and compassion. Being self-controlled will enable us to accomplish our dreams; and it sets the stage for influencing others to achieve their God given purpose in life. Our example will set the stage for great things in our life and in the lives of other people. The verse speaks of encouraging the young men. Our life purpose can be so lived out that we inspire others to achieve their own purpose. Also, an admonition for us to be self-controlled means we should be disciplined to fulfill our vocation or life's calling. We can make godly things happen by the combination of God, our purpose, and others; coupled with vision, and action. Be one who won't settle for second best. Most people's drive dies out when they hit life's continuous petty provocations. We must update our purpose, vision, and thinking regularly. If we settle in and quit setting the pace for ourselves; we end up in mediocre! But if we continue to stir the flame; we can continue to be a life-long achiever.

Our life's conversation should be an example of purpose. Titus 2:7 says, "In everything set them an example by doing what is good. In your teaching show integrity and seriousness." We must exemplify someone who has and exercises our own purpose or mission. If we list our good qualities and sum them up in the top five; then fashion our mission statement for the exercise of our purpose. As we live out our purpose; our life conversation can influence others to greatness. In everything we need to set the example for others. We are the trend setter for the cause of godliness. We must leave them an example. In our teaching we should be those who equip others for the journey of life. We need to do this with integrity and sound judgment. We should do all this with seriousness because our individual purpose is important. If we don't take our work serious; neither will anybody else. The attitude we exercise towards our work is noticed. The danger in a lazy-fair attitude is that it erases the urgency in us and others to fulfill the needs in life. But if we stay focused on our purpose; we will succeed in our work.

Your life's conversation should be an exemplinary life. Titus 2:8 says, "And soundness of speech that cannot be condemned, so that those who oppose you may be ashamed because they have nothing bad to say about us." Our life conversation is the way we fulfill our purpose that God gave us! We must exercise that purpose as to bring glory to Christ so we don't lose our testimony, bring disgrace on Christ, and so others cannot honestly condemn us. The verse speaks of speech that cannot be condemned. People will find fault with us. The verse also speaks of, "those who oppose you maybe ashamed." When we live godly and serve others with our purpose; people will be won by our holy lifestyle or holy conversation: and that brings Satan's rage against us. We need, therefore, to take the time to know how to exercise our purpose and spot opportunities to share our gifts with those who will receive it. The Apostle Paul said that the Corinthians fell behind in no good gift. That was because Paul labored to equip the Corinthian Church. We must be such a leader ourselves. If we discard our purpose and life's conversation; we will ruin our opportunities to influence others for Christ. Let us make sure we walk following Jesus Christ's example. As we follow Jesus example; we will fulfill our purpose by bearing precious fruit.

So, let us carry out our life's conversation by living out our purpose; then our life will be fulfilling and pleasing to God.

YOU HAVE A BUSINESS

What is our spiritual business? Do we know and exercise our purpose? Are we laying hold of opportunities? Knowing our purpose and applying it to our opportunities is our spiritual business. In Philippians 1:9-11 (NIV) we see that we can develop our spiritual business. How can we develop our spiritual business? Let's see how we can develop our spiritual business.

Our spiritual business needs to develop in wisdom and insight. Philippians 1:9 says, "And this is my prayer: that your love may abound more and more in knowledge and depth of insight…" Our business means using our purpose in and through opportunities for God that we accept. It was Paul's desire and prayer for these Christians to be happy and lack in no spiritual gift; but to abound more and more in the knowledge of Jesus Christ; and in the growth and exercise of their faithful use of the gifts God bestowed on them for serving others. Paul told them that was his prayer. This is the Apostles sincere desire for his audience (which includes us) so that our love may abound. If we are so independent so that God cannot bless us; then we cannot bless anybody else. We must abound in the things of God. Paul wanted his hearers to grow and abound exceedingly in the things of God. It takes a mind open to the things of God to be of use by God. When opportunity comes up, we must be ready to exercise ourselves with our faith, gifts, and purpose for service. Are we looking for ways to use our abilities for Gods service? We could spend precious years missing opportunities God sends our way. Let's identify and key into opportunities to use our purpose for the Lord.

Our spiritual business needs to develop in discernment and clarity over the best path. Philippians 1:10 says, "So that you maybe able to discern what is best and maybe pure and blameless until the day of Christ." As we develop character and ability to use our gifts and trade toward Gods cause: we learn to pick the best path and options that God lays before us. We will spot opportunity to bless others and share our faith, gifts and Jesus with others. We must discern what is best. As we exercise our spiritual business; we spot good and bad; and God will give us discernment on how to deal with each issue. So, let us be pure and blameless; then we will find that as we seek to please God; that His power will operate through us. God does not work through unholy vessels. Living pleasing to God is our best option for a life worth living. Let us be always open to possibility to share our faith with our gifts. When we don't develop in our purpose and work, we miss Gods best plan for our lives and others. Avoid slacking in Gods will by developing your practical Christianity every chance you get.

Our spiritual business needs to develop in producing the works of God. Philippians 1:11 says, "Filled with the fruit of righteousness that comes through Jesus Christ-to the glory of Jesus Christ." Gods will be that our lives and business abound in His grace, favor, and help. He is the substance that causes the growth and spiritual fruit to emerge. We need to praise God for producing this fruit by helping us exercise ourselves in Gods purpose and will. Let us be filled with the fruit of righteousness. This is the righteousness that is ours through Jesus Christ by faith in Him. We do all to the glory and praise of God. We always need to remind ourselves to give thanks to God for all things. Our goal is to touch others. But how do we touch others? We touch others by being an open vessel that God works through. Jesus said it is those who do the Fathers will who are the family of God. We must apply our mind and heart to discern what Gods Will is in our situations. We cannot take pop shots to attempt to produce Gods will.

Therefore, we must develop our spiritual business, so our life accomplishes all God put us hear for.

EXERCISING YOUR SPIRITUAL DUTIES

What does working spiritually mean? It means using our gifts to achieve our purpose. It means using our purpose to achieve and accomplish Gods work. We can take advantage of life by using our spiritual trade. In 2 Timothy 4:4-5 (NIV) we see that we can know how to exercise our spiritual duties (our trade.) How can we exercise our spiritual duties? Let's see how we can exercise our spiritual duties.

We can exercise our spiritual duties by abiding in Gods Will. 2 Timothy 4:4 says, "They will turn their ears away from the truth and turn aside to myths." As we exercise our purpose for God's cause within each opportunity we choose to engage in; we will find that there are people with hardened hearts; and they turn away from you to do the will of Satan. We then must make sure we abide in Gods will when we exercise our trade (trade meaning the gifts in our purpose applied to the opportunities to do God's work.) The verse says that they will turn their ears away. People are not going to pay attention to our message; some will, and some won't. We must connect to those who take care to listen. Instead those who turn from us will turn to myths. Many will not head our testimony and example-just let them go. We don't want to be caught in the middle of such defection. We must keep exercising our work (trade) for Jesus Christ's cause. When we work on a job; we don't quit till our shift is over. Keep at it with our spiritual trade in the Lords work all our life; till we cannot work because we are gone. The danger in not pressing on in Gods Will is to succumb to other influences and distractions. Let us take care to abide with God; then we will not stagger in our spiritual duties.

We can exercise our spiritual duties by pressing on amidst resistance. 2 Timothy 4:5a says, "But you keep your head in all situations;

endure hardships." When we are hard pressed; that is not the time for us to give in or give up. That is the time to press on amidst the opposition. We must stay focused; stay the course and keep our mind. Endure patiently. The bible commands us to maintain our walk and keep godly habits. We can endure hardships by pressing on in dark times. When we give up; we lose our reward; don't quit working. If our peers' pressure us; don't quit over it. If we give up our work goes down the drain. But if we press on in a progressive manner; we will be amazed at how God will work through us.

We can exercise our spiritual duties by using them at the max capacity. 2 Timothy 4:5b says, "Do the work of an evangelist, discharge all duties of your ministry." Paul tells Timothy to maintain and excel in putting everything he has, to work for God! Press the ability to its max to obtain the favor of God. We must put our capacities to work by getting it done! Let us make our gifts count! The apostle spoke of doing the work of an evangelist. We must preach and use our trade to spread the gospel. Discharge the duties of our ministry. We each have specific gifts and duties to put into motion to achieve

Gods good will for us. We have no time to lose; we must serve God at max potential. If we have the gifts of help, for example, help as many people as we can. Let us put our gifts to work. If we neglect our duties (opportunities) we may miss the eternal benefits. But it we work we can expect lasting results.

So, know how to exercise your spiritual duties so you can accomplish Gods will for you.

DAILY EXPEND YOURSELF IN YOUR SPIRITUAL BUSINESS

Why should we be fervent in our call? Well, we see that there is a purpose in every endeavor. There is a purpose in learning a discipline in college. There is a purpose for daily laboring on the job. Your spiritual work is essential to your eternal happiness. In Romans 12:11 (KJV) we see that we should exercise our spiritual business daily. But how can we exercise our spiritual business daily? Let's see how we can exercise our spiritual business daily.

We can exercise our spiritual business with zeal. Romans 12:11a says, "Not slothful in business..." This is an admonition to utilize and exercise all godly means in our purpose in the works God provides by opportunity. Opportunity is an appropriate and favorable time or occasion to use our stuff for God. We are commanded to be not slothful. That means we need to exercise zeal in business. It means to be energetic, devoted activity at any work or task; diligence according to the Random House dictionary. The word also says that we should attend to the Lords business. Our business is to fulfill the mission, purpose, and spiritual work God has given us to do at various times in our life; let's not waist our opportunities. Nobody but we can live out our dreams. To fulfill Gods will in our lives is the ultimate fulfillment of our dreams. We must give ourselves permission to do this and allow nothing to stop us from fulfilling our spiritual quest to do the work God appoints for us. Anyone who works on a job has learned skill and a routine to achieve the expectations put upon him: we need to carry out our purpose so we can achieve Gods expectations for us. He expects us to fulfill our purpose in life. Can you imagine missing out in life by living it out without discovering and fulfilling your purpose? It's tragic because our heavenly foundation will be laid on a base without the purpose! So, we must discover and live out our God given purpose; with effort and thought, we can do it.

We can exercise our spiritual fervor. Romans 12:11b says, "Fervent in spirit." Paul urges his listeners to get fervent in their hearts; having a fiery spirit which will not allow its light for God to be put out! The admonition here is for us not only to be in busy service; but to put all our heart into it. To prepare and motivate our own heart means we must stay ready for action. This is in opposition to the carelessness of the world toward the things of God; and it will cause persecution to come on people. The verse says to be fervent. Random House Dictionary defines this as warmth, or intensity of feeling; ardor; zeal; fervor! There are times we have had intensity of feeling. Acquire that feeling and channel it towards achieving your purpose in Gods work. Are we being fervent in our spirits? We allow our spirits to be stirred to activity; in the essence of who we are in God; towards any opportunity He gives us to use our gifts, testimony, and purpose for His cause. We can and should be ready to work at every opportunity with reasonable application.

We cannot do everything; but we can do many things! Let's attempt to do what we can do. How is your fire? If you won't turn up the fuel; your fire won't burn hot and bright; then you'll lack in fulfilling your call! So put the preparation and action into this so you're always ready to serve.

We can exercise our spiritual business with service. Romans 12:11c says, "Serving the Lord." Our commission is to witness to others, baptize them, and disciple them. In other words, influence them to repent and turn to God by faith in Jesus. The object of the fulfillment of our purpose in the great commission is to serve God! I want to mention that we only have a lifetime to discover our purpose; apply it; and use it to serve God in the great commission. And how we have done that lays the foundation for our lives eternally for the time to come after our earthly probationary period is over! We are commanded to serve the Lord. The whole goal of spiritual leadership is to come to the place where we serve others; and God. We serve others and engage in Gods work because God is the object of our faith and service; not the people we serve! Service is the objective of our purpose because God has first loved us! We love and serve others not because of how they treat us but because God has loved us every day of our lives! God, from eternity, has planned out our lives and our realms and bounds of our habitations so that we would come to realize all good we have had been His doing in our lives! So, we might reach out to Him in love and service! The world has it backward. They turn to society to learn a trade; then use that trade to step all over others to climb a ladder of success. God's way is for us to be used up to make sure others lack in no spiritual gift. Which path have we been treading on?

It is therefore essential to our eternal benefit to lay a foundation of service that will suite our purpose in heaven. We must, then, work our purpose and spiritual business to fervently serve God and others to obtain the heavenly goals.

TAKE CARE OVER YOUR WORK

Can the elements of life destroy our work? Unconcerned people could destroy it. Unthoughtful reactions of our own doing may nullify it. We must guard our work and business to continue to bear fruit. In 2 Timothy 2:14-19 (KJV) we see that it is critical that we guard our business. Why should we guard our business? Let's see why we should guard our business.

We must guard our spiritual business by staying clear of quarrels. 2 Timothy 2:14 says, "Of these things put them in remembrance, charging them before the Lord that they strive not about words to no profit, but to the subverting of the hearers." We are to avoid vain arguments; things that bring no edification. Conversations in which slander and gossip are involved we need to stay clear of. It is precisely these things which cause those who engage in it to be overthrown. The verse says to, "Put them in remembrance." We must remind ourselves to avoid useless talk to spare our work in Christ. We are not to strive about words to no profit. That means we need to stop using useless conversation that will ruin our spiritual business. This is so that we avoid the subverting of the listener. This will ruin our own work. Anyone who is seriously attempting to engage in a work for God must avoid unwholesome and negative conversation to spare their own ministries: as well as the listeners. God listens to our conversations! We must do all as unto Him; and that means control our tongue, ears, and mind; and who we converse with, and where we go. Do not take a lazy-fare attitude on your speech. If we talk like an important person; we can avoid the dangers of destroying our own works.

We must guard our spiritual business by staying approved through study. 2 timothy 2:15 says, "Study to show yourself approved unto God, a workman that need not be ashamed, rightly dividing the Word of Truth." It is expected that we will study as spiritual leaders. If we plan on keeping our spiritual work up to speed, we must know the Word. We are commanded to study. We are to set our mind on God's Word; so, we don't have to be ashamed. When we rightly read the Word, we need not be confounded. We must develop the habit to feed anytime we would need to eat spiritually. Our study is a major key in the ability to spot opportunity to do our work. If we won't study our business will come to an end without vision and direction. We must keep the vision current by getting in the book.

We must guard our spiritual business by staying away from false doctrine. 2 timothy 2:16-18 says, "But shun profane and vain babblings: for they will increase unto more ungodliness; and their word will eat like a cancer; of whom is Hymenaeus, and Philetus; who concerning the truth have erred. Saying the resurrection is past already and overthrows the faith of some." If we don't avoid false doctrine, our enemy; those bringing Satan's lies; will overthrow our business by their lies. The lies spoken by such people will destroy our work because it eats like a canker. These persons have erred; so, we must stick to the basic theology; and avoid being overthrown. Satan's aim is to overthrow people's faith. If you build your business on Satan's lies of false assumptions; it will not make it very far. God will destroy those works that are based on lies. Please don't take advice from Satan's collaborators. If you will seek out God and do it His way; you will prosper.

We must guard our spiritual business by staying in a vibrant walk with God. 2 Timothy 2:19 says, "Never-the-less, the foundation of the Lord stands sure, having this seal; the Lord knows them that are His. And let everyone that names the name of Christ depart from iniquity." Our business is only as good as our walk of obedience and being in the favor and fellowship of God. Our walk and fellowship with God is our foundation. Therefore, we must depart from iniquity. If we belong to God, we will stop the sin habit. We, by prayer, can align ourselves to know Gods will; and to carry that will out obediently in life. Prayer is so we can discover and do the will of God. To neglect our walk will dismantle our business. But if we work at it; we will continue to grow into Jesus Christ. Then our work will be a success.

So, we must guard our business from anything that would void it out; that way we can fulfill God's call on our life.

WORKING TO HELP YOUR COMMUNITY

Can we make a difference in our community? We all have something that we can contribute. We all can find someone who needs our help. Knowing our skills and using them to help others will make our community better. In Ephesians 4:11-13 (NIV) we see that we should know how to use our spiritual trade in the community. How do we use our trade in the community? Let's see how we can use our trade in the community.

We need to recognize our position in Jesus Christ. Ephesians 4:11 says, "It was He who gave some to be apostles, some to be prophets, some to be evangelists, and some to be preachers and teachers." We must know what our position of authority is in Jesus Christ. The position of authority is that thing or office God has given us that we have authority in which we have power to operate for Jesus Christ's cause! God has given us an authoritative office. It might be different then the ones mentioned; but we have one and need to know what it is. It was God who gave each of us our gifts and office. Jesus has given each believer an office and authority to live it out on His behalf. The verse mentions such offices as pastor, teacher, etc. It is not limited to such; but whatever our calling might be in which we can use for His work. As we discern our calling and position, we need to begin to look for ways to exercise it for Christ's cause! Use it for the cause of Christ in all settings we are in. We need to especially use our purpose, business, or trade to assist anyone into a relationship with Jesus Christ and His ways in all communities we are in. We must be the beacons of authority for God! We go forward in authority! Not to compete or jostle with other people; but as experts in our call. We go forward in authority as those who use their skills to help others. If we refuse to identify our position (office) of authority and think it insignificant; we will lose precious time applying our skill and authority to make a difference in our community. My friend lets go forward in authority and faith; knowing our gifts and spiritual business; instead of being unsure and lingering in doubt and fear.

We need to recognize the application of our trade. Ephesians 4:12 says, "To prepare Gods people for works of service, so that the body of Christ maybe built up." We are called of God to walk with Him and to be His vessel that uses our abilities, purpose, applications of all our resources in all opportunities we can for Gods cause (our trade.) We do this by serving other people in our community setting. The verse says that God gave these things to prepare Gods people for works of service. An adult raises their children to learn, be, and live responsibly. We use our position and gifts to train others to be an adult who responsibly applies themselves to Gods work in their settings. We do this so the body of Christ maybe built up. Our effort is an attempt to win and disciple prospects to their edification in Christ. We must be aware, always, as to when we can apply ourselves in our settings, as opportunity arises. We only have one lifetime to impact our eternal future as well as others. We must motivate ourselves to action. If we won't invest ourselves into others, then we will lose the possibility of a future role of authority because we were not faithful with the gifts entrusted to us here by God. The application and faithful exercising of our gifts, talents, abilities, purpose, and spiritual business determines eternal roles. We determine our future according to what we do with the Good News. We must not waist our opportunities.

We need to recognize the vision of our goals. Ephesians 4:13 says, "Until we reach unity in the faith and in the knowledge of the Son of God, and become mature, attaining to the whole measure of the fullness of Christ." We will always have to apply ourselves this side of eternity because it is here that we strive for the unity of the faith. Our goal is to continue to work for God until we, and others with our help, reach maturity in Christ. This will be a lifelong goal sense the biggest room in our lives is the room of growth; we will always need to grow more into the likeness of Christ. The scripture is telling us that we exercise ourselves this way until we, "reach unity of faith." Our goal is to bring ourselves to use our all in our work and to assist others to grow and be effective workers for God too! It is never ending; and occurs one person at a time; using our teaching skills. The objective here is for us to contribute to the wellbeing of our communities. We do this in a way people become mature through our work and example and people are growing into the fullness of Christ. As we will see in future messages; this will take both our wholehearted effort and the cooperation and collaboration of ourselves in Jesus Christ to do this. My goal in this series is to unify the effort with vision; each of our own; and collectively applying ourselves in the whole. Today people grope in the dark because they lack purpose and have not seen people of purpose! We must be willing to step in and make a change in ourselves, and others to redirect our efforts for equipping ourselves for the future. God commissions us to edify and equip others in this way.

So, we need to exercise authority in our skill to use our purpose, resources, and work in the community to edify and win it to Christ. We must equip ourselves by preparing our mind and will to do Gods work, and then we will bear fruit.

DISCERN YOUR MISSION AND PURPOSE FROM OTHERS

We are distinct in God's work. We have our own face and features. We have our own responsibilities in life. In God's work we have our own call and work to do. In Romans 12:3-6a (NIV) we see that it is essential for us to exercise our gift according to our measure of faith. Why exercise our gift according to our measure of faith? Let's see why we must exercise our gift according to the measure of our faith.

We must humbly exercise our gift with right motives according to our measure of faith. Romans 12:3 says, "For by the grace given me I say to every one of you: do not think of yourself more highly then you aught, but rather think of yourself with sober judgment, in accordance with the measure of faith God has given you." We are to exercise our gifts in the reverence of God; knowing the gifts originate from Him and not ourselves. The ability we have is the measure of faith God has first given us. According the grace given me; Paul said. We can only do what we can because God allows it. We must not think of ourselves more highly then we aught. Sense God controls it all; we must be humble about our abilities. We must live in sober judgment exercising our gifts always in the light that God has given it to us. It is essential that, as we exercise faith, that we realize that both the faith and gifts are from God. What we possess and all we are is granted to us on loan so we might use it so that the kingdom won't suffer loss. We must do things for Gods glory. We cannot use our gifts for any purposes; it must honor God. Our motive must be to finish Gods assigned work for us and to glorify His name. If we bypass right motives; we may forfeit our reward. Therefore, we must pray and honor God in how we exercise our gifts.

We must humbly exercise our gift without confusing our work and ability with someone else. Romans 12:4 says, "Just as each of us has one body with many members; and these members do not all have the same function..." This verse expresses what must be our goal as members of Christ's body: that each of us has our own purpose and work in Jesus Christ to do. The person(s) who God puts in charge of any group that has gathered to serve in Gods flock has to direct the unity of each person's collaboration towards the goal in the work. The verse says, "As each of us has one body and many members." The body of Christ has many members that have their own purpose; yet function together to do what the body is told to do by the head. This is essential so we don't presume our purpose and calling, or vocation, on other people. An electrician, on a job, serves a different purpose then a carpenter. If we assume others must know our personal mission and demand, they do it our way; we cause others to stumble and contend with one another.

We must humbly exercise our gift with attention on serving God and others. Romans 12:5 says, "So in Christ we who are many forms one body, and each member belongs to all the others." We must discern, within our labor, which is Christ body-those who follow Him; and make it our aim to serve them and God. If possible, we should serve all people if it assists persons to believe the gospel. We belong to one another in Christ: so, we serve the members of His body. It is in Jesus Christ that each member belongs to each other. How do we enforce this belonging? We do so as we serve each other in Christ with love. We are studying this series to know when and who to serve. We serve Gods family and do so as opportunity arises. It is our obligation also to use our potential to win the lost by our testimony, actions, and love! If we are bestowed with gifts but do not serve others; just ourselves; we will fail the reason for our purpose. Let's make place for others in our life.

We must humbly exercise our gift with respect to the fact of it being uniquely our gift by the Holy Ghost. Romans 12:6 says, "We have different gifts, according to the grace given us." This says we have our own gift and it is uniquely our gift! Other persons have their own gift. We skew our vision if we mix our purposes. The verse says we have differing gifts. We don't practice exercising other people's gifts. It would be silly for us to attempt to live out other people's gifts. We are not designed for their gifts. We may even get hurt. Do not emulate the gifts of other people. We have our own and those are the ones God will bless us on.

So, let us exercise our gift according to our faith. Then as we learn to work around other people; let them have liberty to be who they are in Christ; as we be who we are in Christ: and we can live out what Christ calls each of us to.

COMBINED EFFORT

Can we work together in God's business? If we are willing and attempt to build up our relationships with other people, then yes, we can. If we see a need and train ourselves and others to meet that need, then yes, we can. Paul shows the Corinthians Church that together we are set apart for God's service and work. In 1Corinthians 3:5-9 (KJV) we see we can join in business with our fellow workers. How are we able to join in business with our fellow workers? Let's see how we can join in business with our fellow workers.

Each person is gifted with a work that God has given to add value to Gods work. 1 Corinthians 3:5. "Who then is Paul, and who is Apollo's, but ministers by whom ye believed, even as the Lord gave to every man." God has given to each of us something with which we can add value to God's work. We are called to work together in Gods Work. So, the verse says, "Who is Paul or Apollo's?" In Christ we each are those that are Gods instruments which He works through to do His bidding. We are like ministers who do Gods work according to our gifts. Just as, "the Lord gave to everyman." We also have an office, authority of some capacity, and something to use for Gods work. We must spot opportunity and join in as God opens doors. In Soul Winning; we must exercise the gifts by the Spirits leading; and use our gifts to win souls to God: that is Gods work. We take initiative to incorporate others into the work. We train them through befriending them. This is discipleship on the individual level. If we won't do that; we won't bear fruit and they won't grow.

Each person contributes in their own unique way. 1 Corinthians 3:6 says, "I have planted, Apollo's watered, but God gave the increase." Whether persons work the same shifts and times; or one comes after the other: each person has their own job to do in Jesus Christ. But each must do his or her part to win the lost to God without nullifying the work of the other; remembering that we all work for the Lord. Paul said that, "I have planted." Paul won the people to Christ. Then he said, "Apollo's watered." Apollo's edified and built up the people in Christ. Finally, "God gave the increase." The harvest came from God; therefore, we ought to focus on our own responsibilities before God. Each person has their own work and we aught to trust God for our part of the harvest. I cannot dictate to a brother or sister what they should do; nor should they do so to me; but as I follow Christ, it is God's Will that I do what Jesus tells me to do. The danger is that we neglect our part. If we work diligently, we will experience harvest. We will then see that our effort and work have impact.

Each person along with the working group depends on God for the harvest. 1 Corinthians 3:7 says, "So then, neither him that planteth anything, neither he that watereth; but God that giveth the increase." We must come to grips with balance. Yes, our part is important; but in the scope of the work, it is Gods work and sovergn hand that matters. Without Gods help we can do nothing. The verse uses the word, "anything." We are only able to do a work if God will allow us to. It goes on to say that God gives the increase. God has given the abilities, gifts, and administrations that make the work possible and workable; we must thank Him and give Him glory. We are like a useless light fixture with no electricity: if we don't have God we cannot not shine. Therefore, the harvest is by Gods power. We must work with and trust God or we won't get a return on our work. We don't want to labor for nothing. Let us acknowledge Gods help in all that we do.

Each person will be rewarded for doing their part. 1 Corinthians 3:8 says, "Now he that planteth and he that watereth are one; and everyman shall receive his own reward according to His own labor." Each of us is given a work and the great commission. And we are to be unified and in one purpose in the work. If we are faithful, we will be rewarded for our part. The verse speaks of us being one. We share the gospel and we are together unified in the work. Then it goes on to say that each receives his or her own reward. We will be rewarded for our part in the work. This is exciting! At the Bema judgment or accountability day we will receive our reward. We should stir up our initiative to do Gods work then. Paul speaks of stirring up the faith; while James says we are to put our faith to work. How can we get our reward if we won't do anything? If we apply ourselves with others; we will receive a return.

Each person is Gods worker in His field which do Gods work. 1 Corinthians 3:9 says, "For we are laborers together with God; ye are Gods husbandry; ye are Gods building." This verse speaks of God, you, me, and all Jesus Christ's followers as unified in Gods work. Can we change our thinking, hearts, and attitudes about our fellow workers; so that together we get Gods work done? We are laborers together. Together we work God's field. We are Gods husbandry or building. We are Gods work in which He demonstrates to the world to woe them to Him. We are Gods building in which He uses to bring glory to Himself. Jesus says the field is already white unto harvest-it's ready to be harvested. When harvest comes, we together, get in the field and get it done; we don't fight one another. There cannot be a harvest if we won't join Gods people in the field. If we are laborers together then we will have to get in the mud and get dirty. If we be willing to work; God will do a work through us by causing us to bear fruit.

Join in the work of God along with our fellow Disciples of Christ. When we team up with others; much more can be accomplished.

WE CAN COMMUNICATE DIGNITY TO OTHERS

How can we give ourselves to others? We can be available to share our gifts and person. We also can respond with care to those who need us. We can practice what we learn by helping other people as we were taught. In 1 Thessalonians 3:11-13 (KJV) we see that it is critical we exercise the purpose of our communication. Why must we exercise the purpose of our communication? Let's see why we must exercise the purpose of our communication.

We must exercise the purpose of our communication by using our gift to build others up in fellowship. 1 Thessalonians 3:11 says, "Now God Himself and our Father, and our Lord Jesus Christ, direct our way unto you." Paul prayed that God would so direct their path that they could come to the people in a way that Paul could show them love toward one another. Our goal is to so exercise leadership that we build up the fellowship where none are neglected. The verse expressed that it is Gods Will that we communicate His love to edify by using our gifts, purpose, work, trade, business, and unity in Gods work. When the verse says, "direct our way unto you;" it is an expression meaning we must cooperate with Gods intent to go forth to others to edify them. The goal in Gods work is not for us to acquire self security through inordinate self preservation, but to be secure enough to help other people. We should consider and take to heart the value of others in Gods eyes: that is why He gave us all that we have; so that we can help other people. It seems to be that if we obtain a skill, gift, ability and resources; that it will disappear over time if we won't exercise it for Gods work. We need to be sure we use our things for Gods work by building others up in faith.

We must exercise the purpose of our communication by using our gift to add value to others. 1 Thessalonians 3:12 says, "And the Lord make you to increase and abound in love one toward another, and toward all men, even as we do toward you?" Paul left us an example that we should exercise our work together toward adding value to other people; those of faith and the unbelieving who open to our hospitalities; to the intent of increasing and abounding toward one another in love. Paul said, "The Lord make you increase." It is Gods will we increase in using our things in cooperation to build and give value to others. It goes on to say, "Even as we toward you." We love it when there are those who add value to our lives; but why can't we do so to others? All we must do to add value to others is to stay open to opportunity to share ourselves with those in need. We must not pass up a person who needs our resources. If we refuse to use our resources to assist others; we may lose them permanently. We must use your gifts; or lose them through disuse. In God, the more we serve by giving away ourselves and gifts; the more God blesses us.

We must exercise the purpose of our gift to strengthen other people's hearts. 1 Thessalonians 3:13 says, "To the end He may establish your hearts unblamable in holiness before God, even our Father, at the coming of our Lord Jesus Christ with all His saints." Paul encourages us to establish each others' hearts in faith in God using our gifts, purpose, and work. The verse speaks of establishing the audience in holiness; we aught to work together in Gods work, being strong, in spiritual excellence in God. It goes on to speak of the coming of the Lord. It addresses Christ's coming so that we prepare for that day by laboring in Him so that we will have a good account to give. Let's focus on bringing people to a place of stability and usefulness in faith. The whole purpose of God giving such gifts, work, and authority is so that we are a repose and example to others. Be not like some who neglect to help others with their God given abilities. Let us refocus off self to the needs of others; then we will be instrumental in their healing and growth.

So, know that the purpose of our communication is to serve others in the work God gives us to do. Then, as we carry out our mission, we will build others up in a great way.

HONOR GOD IN ALL YOU DO

How can we honor God in all our endeavors? We can be hospitable in our communications. We can imitate Jesus in our lifestyle and conduct. Our life should be acceptable to God. In Romans 12:1-2 (NIV) we see we can honor God in all ways. How can we honor God in all ways? Let's see how we can honor God in all ways.

We can honor God by being a living sacrifice to Him. Romans 12:1 says, "Therefore, I urge you, brothers; in view of Gods mercy; to offer your bodies as living sacrifices, holy and pleasing to God; which is your spiritual act of worship." In the work in which we offer ourselves and all goody-goody things; from which we must work a good work: we are called to be a living sacrifice in which we offer our all to God. But the offering of ourselves should be holy and pleasing to God. This is the demand of spiritual service. Paul urged his listeners; and it is my pleasure to express to you the urgency before us. We are to offer our bodies in spiritual worship to God. God expects us to do things by His leading and His Word. We should live in a pleasing way to God. We all, who engage in a spiritual work, are called to use all we are and must impact others for Christ. We need to use all opportunities we can to do so. By knowing and practicing our gift, we will honor God. That is the exercise of our lives that God expects from us. Its fine living for God but if we never do anything with the gospel that is not acceptable. If living for God is unacceptable to us, then our life is not a living sacrifice for God. Let us think about the opportunities before us and tackle them. Our life will be worthwhile living for God this way.

We can honor God by avoiding the patterns of this world. Romans 12:2a says, "Do not conform any longer to the pattern of this world but be transformed by the renewing of your mind." If we will honor God; we must set out to please Him at the outset of the day; adjusting our thoughts for reaching Gods goals at the very beginning. So, we don't conform to the world which results in forsaking Gods plan because it does not allow us to achieve the good results. We are transformed by spending time with God; and we become fruit bearers. Holiness is conducive to good fruit bearing. Fruit bearing honors God. We need to make sure we avoid worldliness by spending time with God. If we neglect holiness; we won't bear fruit at all; but God will chastise us until we get back on the path.

We can honor God by approving Gods good Will on all occasions. Romans 12:2b says, "Then you will be able to test and approve what Gods Will is-His good, pleasing, and perfect will." Those words all mean the same thing; that to do Gods will acceptably, by serving God and others in all our abilities. We can live a God approving lifestyle which will prove Gods Will to those observing at all times. The verse declares that we can test and approve what is good. When we know our purpose; we can discern people's motives by how they act and what they do. By living out our spiritual trade for God we will win others to Gods cause. We should work at this some everyday until its second nature to us.

By practicing our gifts for God; we are living set apart for God. It is a sad testimony to dishonor God by refusing to honor him by not working for Him; we show that grace brings change.

Honor God in all ways to prove the necessity for the gifts God has given you; and others will praise God because of your confidence.

Printed in the United States
by Baker & Taylor Publisher Services